Wild Evolution

Wild Evolution
© Naomi Leimsider / Cathexis Northwest Press

No part of this book may be reproduced without written permission of the publisher or author, except in reviews and articles.

First Printing: 2023

ISBN: 978-1-952869-61-5

Cover Image by Annie Spratt @ anniespratt.com
Editing & Design by C. M. Tollefson
Cathexis Northwest Press

cathexisnorthwestpress.com

Wild Evolution

Poems:
Naomi Leimsider

Cathexis Northwest Press

For Joel & Zoë

Table of Contents

Part I: Life Cycles in the Anthropocene

Half-Life	1
Virus Child	2
Creation Play	3
Sex Fat	4
Vestalia	5
Wild Evolution	7
Late Hour	8
Microchimera	9
The Call of the Void	10
Physical System	11
In the Evening, During Quarantine	12

Part II: Afflictions & Conditions

Virus Poem	17
In the Morning, After a Fever Breaks	18
The Kissing Disease	19
Quotidian Fever	20
Gone Toxo	21
In Native State	22
Unscientific Study	23
Animal Rain	24
The Endling	25
Hummers	26
Catatonia	27
Abulia	28

Part III: Short History

Lesson	33
Pure O	34
Strangertwin	35
Advanced Math	36
Open Poem to My Grifter	37
Pact	38
Conundrum	39
Polymath Girl Poem	40
Flat Space	41
Crazy For Two	42
Origin Story	43

We say that only the things of the present exist: the past no longer exists and the future doesn't exist yet. But in physics there is nothing that corresponds to the notion of "now". Compare "now" with "here". "Here" designates the place where the speaker is: for two different people 'here' points to two different places. 'Now' also points to the instant in which the word is uttered.... But no one would dream of saying that things 'here' exist, whereas things which are not 'here' do not exist. So then why do we say that things that are 'now' exist and that everything else doesn't? Is the present something which is objective in the world, that 'flows' and that makes things 'exist' one after the other, or is it only subjective, like 'here'?

Seven Brief Lessons on Physics
Carlo Rovelli

"Now, don't be frightened, loves," Mrs. Whatsit said. Her little body began to shimmer, to quiver, to shift. The wild colors of her clothes became muted, whitened. The pudding-bag shape stretched, lengthened, merged. And suddenly before the children was a creature more beautiful than Meg had even imagined, and the beauty lay in far more than the outward description. She was a marble-white body with powerful flanks, something like a horse but at the same time completely unlike a horse, for from the magnificently modeled back sprang a nobly formed, torso, arms, and a head resembling a man's, but a man with a perfection of dignity and virtue, an exaltation of joy such as Meg had never before seen.... From the shoulders slowly a pair of wings unfolded, wings made of rainbows, of light upon water, of poetry.

A Wrinkle in Time
Madeleine L'Engle

Part I:
Life Cycles in the Anthropocene

Half-Life

When I explain to my daughter that she has eggs inside her; in fact,
a whole regulated cracker jack system, perfectly suspended in the pocket
of her star stuff, waiting for a shuffle to set off the static shock that is the hormone
cascade of the shape shift between small child and wild adult, she is floored,
of course, but she gathers her courage, deftly uses her newly gifted language,
and asks me, her biological mother, with great scientific precision:
not like the eggs we scramble in the pan? not like the eggs we use to bake a cake?
not like the cold eggs we use to turn one thing into another?

Part of my job is to share stories of the remarkable world. My daughter
is innocent to my radioactive griftress, graftress, con woman history. My spinner
of marvelous partial tales ways: I am unreliable on my best day. But I am supposed
to be her narrator, so I try to reduce my lies by half. I can give her this one honest
moment: no, not like those eggs. Your eggs are hot eggs; your eggs live in the quantum
world; your eggs might someday power up for the zinc spark; your eggs are pinpoints
of light blinking secret code into the curve of time.

My daughter already tells herself all the stories of the universe: how we hold
the future inside ourselves, the why and way of decay, that we lose the horizon
flying miles above the sea. She is still full of lightning, so she does not consider
how quickly we lose electricity. She only questions the frenzy, the alchemy:
how does the magic energy of our eggs spontaneously turn elements into us?
are we assigned an egg at the beginning of time? will there be another egg
like our egg again?

I run up against truth. The chaos of lines drawn and redrawn, the hum of mad
uncertainty, how it is all goes unstable. Mother substance decays into daughter
substance: daughter substance gives no quarter. I dance around explanations, definitions,
the how of how it is. I already miss the halcyon days of my old slippery ways when I
could spin several slick stories at once, soften the edges, make it sweet, easy to swallow,
soothe with half lies; tell her we are meant to be, things happen for a reason, there is full
free will. But I should practice my skills, hone newfound honesty: some eggs are better
than others, some eggs start good and go bad, some eggs are always rotten.

I swear I knew her face long before her egg bubbled up, pulsed, ripened. Back when
she was still independent of her physical state. This can only be true in the half-hidden
reality of absolute time before she became my daughter. There is no way to explain
transition and survival in a world where eggs exist, begin, break down, the deep truth
that once life has begun an organic body cannot slake its thirst for disintegration.

How can I tell her there are places on my earth that cannot be inhabited again
for millennia.

Virus Child

My virus child, not even close to full grown, plays virus princess on the dying summer beach, bending the wilderness of virus kingdom to her will. She strains the salt out of the ocean, guts sea creatures in the crashing surf, builds castles in the middle of muddy wave pools so any fellow monarch can shelter behind makeshift moats. All those unable to shed their old-world shell and find a home in this novel, wild land become hapless hosts for shape-shifter switchers on the brink of spillover and will be buried whole in the dirty sand. This is adaptation at its finest; there is no fresh water or controllable fire or magical medicine anywhere in virus world. Evolution works in myriad ways.

My virus child has never been this powerful. She has arrived in this first new moment of natural selection and rules with a small iron fist; there will be sacrifice, offerings, in the virus years ahead. All must suffer the eventual loss of evolutionary leftovers, the consequences for what can't be gleaned. This virus princess, my only royal issue, grew in this body, my only body, but I will never know the taste of her task. I am caught in the mouth of this moment: soft-bodied, toothless, out of my shell; in thrall to the dank smell of moist predators, the sharp bite of dangerous fish, the rogue waves beating the shifting shore of the giant virus sea.

My virus child will never be free. Not one more unfettered moment. The gloaming comes and goes; it is night on the beach. Virus time moves forward toward a dimmed future. She yearns for chilled milk, bath before bed, a lost story: even virus princesses remember what came before the end of time. The sun will set after this summer; the sky will darken so she can finally sleep. All her subjects threaten mutiny. A potential coup etched in her mind, she is exposed to the rougher elements of restless virus stress. The crowned virus princess speaks in her regal virus dream: don't worry, virus mother queen, the years are still stretched out until death.

Creation Play

A ball of cells is only life if it wants to be.
Thrusting mouthless monster
life; a howling hole of energy.
It floats above and below gravity. It understands nothing
of time and millennia. This perversion
in the universe is awaiting orders.

We are one second before midnight
in the grand clock of things and all the choices
made on our behalf bring us to this very minute.
The insistence of conception. Chromosomal confusion
then a person-shaped speck. A sea star straining
to push limbs out of new sockets. Primordial life always needs
a sticky place to rest its shapeless head. Everybody needs a home,
especially a fresh tangle of metastasizing body parts.
Cells split and divide split and divide.
Blood fills the four chambers of the heart;
thoughts spill into three parts of the mind;
oxygen for two soft, spongy lungs;
taste buds line one muscular tongue.
Born whole human half human a near miss missed or missing
or born still. The agony of pulling dirt from the earth. The phantom pain
of not knowing the future.
Time spent. Bodies loved. All the bones
buried in the ground. Take it all in before the extinction.
There is no greater love than the love of worship,
so get on your knees.

If you let them, they will take parts of you. You might
even ask for it. You might
even want it. You won't know
what you've given away. You denied
yourself many possible futures. You never
listen and you never learn. You do not know
how to love, how to worship,
so what will you do.

Sex Fat

There's this thing called sex fat which needs fat feeds on fat
this sex fat requires fat
so what to do?
You must get fat, so you'll be fat —
calorically dense, that is.
Let me show you how it works!
Let me show you a thing or two!
After all, what else can we do but put on our sloppy shoes and slide
like it's oily then slick trick trip right on through just to get things moving.

You haven't lived until you've needle jabbed your own fat.
Punctured though the surface to the subcutaneous, then the shady visceral wrapped around
your insides like a snake all alive and scaly and cold.
Have you ever gone all light-headed and crazy dizzy, you know, a little loopdy-doo and giggly, too?
Do you know how to push deep, deep to the deltoid right through to the sinew?
Intramuscular: it even sounds like it hurts.

Well, you wanted it, now you've got it galore!
Yellow-blue bruised and fatty fat now, it's your engine now, what turns you on now, all that supple mouthfeel now
how now yearning, how now desire, how now motivation, how now lust
and the future!
White fat, brown fat, pale goose bumpy veiny chicken fat, turn you inside out fat, gristly umami fat, between your teeth fat, suck the fucking marrow fat, get sloppy fat
so now you have plenty of sex fat.

I mean
you hope! Who knows how this sex fat thing actually works? It's so confusing
all this is is this sex fat or is this sex fat or is this sex fat or is this?

But this is all good news, so celebrate your small victory!
You're on your way now
you've come back in style now. Everyone can see
you've been making a habit of this.
So put on your sex jacket and gear up for another round
you're so plump and ready you are now.

Vestalia

I dance all night in bloody June, but conception is not as easy as promised
in unlucky June.
Hearth and home, fresh eggs, and all things supposedly growing, blooming
in fertile June.
The season of something sent but never received has just begun, yet it is already
coming to an end over and over and over again
in restless June.
There are only four weeks and once it's done it's done. Another year gone.
The desperate way a body craves babies, but sometimes there is only
salted rain and the clotted clouds
of gloom June gloom.

One by one they are not born. One by one they are expelled into the great
garbage shoot in the sky. Space dust, star stuff, gods disappeared
in smoke.
Frozen feet tucked under unformed knees dug into dribs and drabs of stomach
missing chin into chest. Blood is for spring cleaning. What goes up
must come down.
Look!
The sky is raining.
There should be stillness, bowed heads, many moments of silence, but no —
so merciless June.

I am told there will still be offerings.
Sacrifice — yes, of course — but also meats, fruits, and cakes. Such strange harvest
this June.
There are empty chairs at the table. Come sit down.
Consume.

The cake is not hard-baked, so I stuff my face with it. Light, soft, punishingly
sweet. I chew charred meats dipped in savory sauce for easy swallowing. I eat
so much fruit my stomach is rounded with ripe flesh and seeds -- the wrong kind
of life -- but I take what I can get.

I decide I must shed my human skin but

I am not the immortal king's daughter
I cannot keep fire burning
I cannot keep water from the ground
I have never been a virgin
I am not a goddess of anything.

It's coming for me, yes, it's coming for me and
I cannot wait, no, I cannot wait for another August.
Another summer gone. Another cold fall coming.

And then the dream. I remember the dream. It was June. Always and always year
after year.
A wall of rocks disconnecting me from the world with just a tummy of swollen light
peeking through and grass way too green. Nothing real except
the deer with liquid eyes.
Life, I told it. Here you are. The giver and taker of life. It knows what I know
and there is so, so much pity for me.
It is my shape-shifting bargain, and I must hold up my end.
Okay, fine
but first give me more and more meat over bones, fat loosening under skin,
teeth slipping out of their pulpy seats, nose spreading, organs giving way, and,
at long last, the tell-tale lightning strike of blue veins.
Then I will give you all that I am, all that I know, even what I haven't discovered yet:
that is part of it, too.

But no —
I am handed a bow and arrow I have never shot, and I murder with uncanny precision.
Nobody told me how good it would feel, but there is no time to enjoy
revelation. I must play mother. I must mitigate suffering; I must
embrace the work ahead. I remove
my dress, rip it into ribbons, wrap tourniquets round and round. I put my
dry pink mouth on the wound and suck out the poisoned metal, the septic blood,
the deepening infection.
It was the least I could do.

No, I am not your mother.
Anywhere else this is cause for great disturbance, but it doesn't matter here:
every month is June.
There were other choices I could have made, but no —
I let all of you die, yes, all of you died, will die, after I conceive you
again and again and again.

Wild Evolution

who's been keeping you alive minute after minute. your embryonic body
stuck between necessary -- essential -- phases. you who are hot under the eyes
and in your teeth: a constant low-grade fever is dangerous. sick from the start
you have sunk into the dirty earth.
only twenty days past, and it is already time to crawl back to the cave,
the site of your wild evolution.
your bones exhausted, given in to gravity, become nothing more than all
the kicked-up dust in the world.

Late Hour

There is still plenty of sheer chance left for me in the world. In a universe dying to be born, even a false form can be a future home. Maybe statistics mean little in the face of so much space.

How I long for a body! Just to hold slippery organic matter in my hands, feel it do its slipping, pulsing, thumping thing. Lungs up. Hips long. Abdomen heavy, low. Notice breath. Notice bones. Assess stress. Assess balance. Big tolerance for spiking temperature, the flow of change, many kinds of pain.

Take me back to the energy of the beginning. Remember the solid structure of all those days of stunning beauty one after the other. Reach back and time curves. Reveal that last year was the last year I knew anything at all. Remind me of what's going on beyond a hard no for the future, equations that won't work in my favor. It could still go either way. This is how it is: the past always falls away.

I've lost my mind before. The intimate connection with the fabric of my space is delicate, porous, but I'm in this for the long haul. I am serious, but there's been significant restriction here. At this late hour, when, finally, consent is freely given, my default is still to be so, so quiet, and also refuse to listen. It seems I need to walk around the world before the lesson comes clear: there is loss, but I am right here.

Perhaps I will not last long enough to see this through. Every night I take off my face and see what can be salvaged, what remains. In all probability, the multiple organs and strings of muscular things that make up this mostly functioning form are past the point of practice. So I go incognito: the trick is to blend better, so no one can see you.

I squeeze into a small pocket of time in this space between stops. Not a second spared, not a minute wasted. The last available universe ups the ante; makes me work for it.

Microchimera

I am full of absorbed cells and deep pits of tissue and future tumors and still
it is hard for you to understand: you only exist because of this phenomenon.
Existence is improbable – yours and mine – but still you roam within at cell-level
and grow your trespassed roots inside of me.

How fast I am changing!
Your compulsion to shape shift turns me part animal and the animal part me.
Half-formed, we evolve and evolve and evolve again. Keep the big change moving,
my little changeling: there is my monster face, there is your alien face, there is my
serpent's tail, there are your dragon eyes.

At first you were my guide down the path.
You helped me shudder into existence. You gave me the sleek, muscular body
of a seasoned carnivore and the scalloped tongue and pretty white teeth of a girl.
You learned so fast to develop a taste for the gamey consistency and musty mouthfeel
of my kill. You admire my goatish hungry body. All of my heads. The way I breathe fire
and burn the world. Groom me; brush my lion mane.

Are you mine or am I yours?
You've been with me since the beginning. Protecting me from the fault line. From the first,
the sixth, the ninth swells of shame. Migrating to injury sites. Soothing my wounds.
We are fused, webbed, folded together. Stitched up one side and down the other. You know
me better than I know myself – so tell me, what will I become?

The Call of the Void

"He whose eye happens to look down into the yawning abyss becomes dizzy. But what is the reason for this? It is just as much in his own eyes and in the abyss…"

Kierkegaard

I can only handle the call with gritted teeth precision. Only the organized chaos of surgical intervention and the clean lines of the scalpel path will do in moments like these: the red light of the rules barely holds me back. In a high place, the rubbery band of atmosphere almost pulls away. The urge to spider-climb the how many steps from the abyss staircase up a slippery wall. Swing up before the deep drop down from branch to sky to branch at the top of the world. The tense cling to the desperate waves of some ocean -- any ocean -- until the sick in the small of my stomach kicks in. I'm fine to take a punch, but I can't shake the push of the call, the frantic high frequency pitch ringing danger in both my boxed ears. You can cold spoon my eyes and truss my head up tight, but here I am, like I've always been, about to sink into the pure pressure to give in. It's so much, always too much, but it's the only way I feel love.

Physical System

The night before your death, I realize you are not lucky. There is no other explanation.
I climb into your bed and wrap myself — a bit of my luck of the draw — around your physical
system. The room falls away; nothing else matters. There is little left of you,
just a light-filled shell, but your machine still hums along.

Already you have no definite position, but you are somewhere — here, for example —
and also nowhere at all. I, however, continue to move smoothly through space, cruising my
constant angle, surfing the curve to everywhere I'm going. As luck would have it,
I am nothing if not gifted with trajectory, with forward motion.

In a past life, I swore up and down you'd outlive us all. Me and my false promises.
I used to mark time in the relationship between now and later, but there is no later now.
In this moment, the luck of matter, energy, and information in your shrinking world powers
the last of your system; in the next, indescribable transformation.

Once you were young, but of course you kept on. There is no other choice. Blindsided
by luck, by time, I move from the present to the future. When I touched you, you
were still the single most complex entity in the embedded existence of your environment:
You were there. And I knew it was coming, but I can barely bear the weight of it.

In The Evening, During Quarantine

I
In the spring evening of the future City, I am reminded that me and you and
everyone else, too, has, at one time or another, wished for death. Nothing like
a novel wave of plague to make my dance with dangerous desires, that yearning
for a touch of the pox, go into remission -- yours, too, I'll wager -- because now we
must join our post-medicine world with the return of the merciless medieval reality
that everything is caused by curses. We are still early in the lying-in period, the first
and last forty days of our lives; however, the only choice left is to stoop low enough
to negotiate an ill-conceived bargain with a lesser demon. In spite of this, I know my
turn is coming, so I hang a freshly painted plague cross on the door, splash vinegar
behind boundary stones to ward off virus vectors, spill sand and salt to mark time.

II
A modern hypochondriac in recovery reverts to form in the false comfort
of home on the roof of the City when the plague comes knocking. Winter might
be over, traditionally the sick season of bacteria crossing the oceans on the backs
of rats or in the cells of sailors scared by angry monsters on ancient maps -- the
creatures you meet at sea will surprise you -- but this year brand new similar symptoms
wax and wane with the super sugar moon. I am not steeped in the archaic practice
of pulling on a spicy herbed beak mask to avoid the miasma of plague air, the strange
sweet scent of sloughing skin and rotting, collapsing tender organs. I am not familiar
with the fire damaged breath of dragons. The world will begin again in the fresh warm
morning for some of us, just a lucky few, but maybe not me or you.

III
The woman I was a few hundred years ago has her front door sealed by erstwhile
friends, long-time neighbors in frightened fever pitch: home becomes a pesthouse.
The dreaded locked in period spells the end. There is nothing left to do but pretend
all is well. In this time, mothers go through the motions, the sad charade, of starting
dinner for infected daughters -- my husband already dead in the family bed, maybe
yours, too -- but there is no cold meat or warm bread or ripening fruit. A new plan:
we will convert, become fasting girls, our holy hunger purifying our incubating bodies,
our sickened thoughts. After this, our burials; a kind, immune stranger brings us back
to the earth. The world ceases to exist for us, but in another, later, spring, our empty
house, the streets of our City, will, somehow, fill again.

IV
Centuries later, in the City evening, before the onset of the dark sap spring sky,
I hold a model of modern disease in my future hands. Its sharp spikes stick in
the veiny meat of my unblemished, underworked late humankind palms, and I try
to pierce its organic fat jacket with my fingernails filed to perfect pricking points,
painted bloody pustule black. Forty days earlier, I demanded immortality – you also
were promised you would outlive us all – but we are ancient, the curve of time beyond
our grasp. Watch us conjure potions, create powders of life, to heal post-modern bodies.
Watch the pockmarked sky get dark, settle down. The world falls apart every night,
shapes of it landing all around. We are buried under it but get a reprieve every day.
And I am, you are, somehow, alive, and still alive and still alive and still.

Part II:
Afflictions & Conditions

Virus Poem

In the twilight sleep between alive and not alive, the zombie
twitches to life. Suddenly, it is spiked mouthless muscular hunger,
all jacked up and vascular. Protein-famished, it devours the meatiest
strands then sheds, sheds, its swollen-sized slippery self, feverish
with shape-shift, with mutation. Watch it radicalized by the heady, reckless
call for colonization, the short, sharp cry of imperialism, the nationalist
desire for multiplication! Next is the massive march on its merry, merry
host, who, after a lull, presents with a lump, an alien ache, in the throat:
the things that happen to flesh and blood bodies.

In the Morning, After a Fever Breaks

The world comes back. How lucky! The body cycles through learned
centuries of fever seasons to sweat through its chest, its neck, calm
the soreness of overstretched systems, the deep shivers, the ache
of shaking chills.

How hard the heart knocks around in its cell. How determined
the brain to root out, destroy the deadly mimic within. How suddenly
the body narrows itself to a fault, to a myopic apocalyptic vision,
reduced to a single way to function.

It doesn't exist easily. The body. It assesses how much damage
the imposters can do, expels dead matter through a meatus or two,
yet finds itself running up against it, smack in the middle of it,
somehow, submerged in the false hot world of it.

Who controls what becomes of the body? After a bad night, it will
still carry broken bits of the intruders inside itself for future recognition,
come back for peak hour, all cool and collected, revved up, ready
to live. And it gives and gives and gives.

The Kissing Disease

After the old-fashioned necking, the sore lips, the mouth invasion, it slipped me a mickey, replaced bits of me with itself, brought me to heel. It was nothing if not charming before the damage done, but in the full fog of drugged tender organs and triggered cells, it chewed me into holes, denuded my soil, scorched my earth.

On the other side of my conversion, the sequela hits hard. I cannot still be alive with necessary somethings -- cells, strands, molecules – rearranged, maybe missing. Too much drag on the body, which can handle the shock of small punishments, but notes every slight and violation, every canceled contract.

I'm supposed to watch to see when and what happens. Wait for the break down, the shake out. In the third quarter phenomenon, I find myself in thrall to the way it doesn't joke around, floored by its mercurial self: the way it relishes opportunity, wishes the wild universe dirty, knows nothing beyond itself.

I wonder if the world will forgive me. Such fresh hell for flaunting young round cheeks, biting pretty neck skin bruised, exposing wayward lush flesh.

Quotidian Fever

Two spikes a day; the heat slams through me.
Doubles down, bends around, catches sudden and quick. Then nothing breaks
except the chill of space.
This is how it starts, how it moves.

Somewhere on the spectrum, I am in rhythm with all the hours in the day.
After all, there is no heat like the heat of expanding
and no cold like the cold of exploding.
Only the big body of the universe can bring me back to center.

I am so silly, so small.
I have not defied time or age. Just left out in the sun
too long. The curve behind me now,
pulled back and back to deep time,
and then fast forward,
headlong
into the madness of the future.

Whatever I do, the hot world remains: it will make more of me,
all it wants is to make more of me.

Gone Toxo

i'm the mouse who sniffs the cat to get switched on. my little body aches
to bursting and i dream of going in-cat with only nibbling teeth
to guide me; my poked-out eyes cannot lead the way.

does my crazy make parasite and the cat?
i am beholden to the bodies of both-- benevolent dictators and loving moms –
but the beast never knows he's bitten.
i see smoky eyes, feel twitchy ears, smell sour cat gut, and I am born again.
attracted like a fallen from grace gutter mouse,
reduced to a gray knotted fur bitten off tail growl no cheese howl,
so just put me out with the garbage at the end of Cat Road!
after all,
a tadpole becomes a frog but never snuggles in a snake's shedded skin,
a caterpillar becomes a butterfly but doesn't yearn for the jacamar's mouth --
and you think a mouse doesn't know she's lost her mind?

the beast wants me tasting close
because i am the milk of a cat dream.
my thumpy heart only beats for the beast's psychopath stare,
his still stalking body.
the parasite whispers sweet nothings to me
in the night
in the dark
telling me what to do
what I want next.

in native state

in native state, I wait
in the enormous world of your body
for the sequence of big bang events to unfold.

observe me in native state. watch me into existence
through your microscope, pray over wishing cups. You beg for a mitochondria shake
or two, but I am not a sorceress of sorts or a great fixer of your small universe.

listen to me in native state. I go on and on about sacrifice, how you don't always
get what you want. The unexplained is always idiopathic, but the result is the same:
your ballooning heart broken with news.

this is my final report:
I'll do the violence, the wanting, the killing. Keep me
charged this way, tight with tension, lying in wait.

Unscientific Study

I grew a crown of thorns overnight. Woke up thorny with a sour greenish taste in the back of my old sore throat. Stiff and stuck and jagged around my head, but also, strangely, on all sides, metastasized up and down both thighs. Examined said protuberances -- spiny, spiked, surprisingly slippery – in the hard silence of early morning. Extent of the big change noted for future reference: the suddenness of being invasive in my own space, possible points of entry, how deep red rooting of potentially poisonous growths influences relationship with place. However, little was revealed about how this could happen to my living body. This much I know: we don't get different bodies every season for a reason. Of all the unlucky things to happen! My current predicament (like all my predicaments) must be a bellwether for something or punishment for previously unmentionable things.

What comes next is probably the old story of being shunned, shut out, lest I shed, or spread my new internal tissue, and the inevitable soft rot, around. Someone will find me. See me like this. I'll get pulled, crushed, or cut up – like rotting vegetables or diseased weeds – reduced to crawling on thorny hands and knees licking the salty, dirty, woody ground. No other opinions necessary now: those well-versed in this line of work would be looking for reasonable answers of their own. Or just want to yank me out, chop me down. Who knows what will feel good after this, but it is certainly not the flash warning of aura, tense moments of dizzying nausea, then the woozy drowsiness that seems to cause these thorns to grow, twist, and form into (what appears to my still novice eye) a permanent prickly halo of red light, which does not bode well for me who still wants to live through all the coming days into all the coming nights.

I need to be replanted. Find a way to accommodate, propagate, thrive. Before this, I was just living: clearing away evidence, hiding old lies deep inside the punishing ground, steeped in despair over prizes lost, money not won, days wasted waiting for the sharp turn of luck that won't likely come. When the wild world wakes up, rouses itself from (what I already remember as) delicious guileless sleep, and closes in, it will discover, as I did, the cost of getting caught, how many mistakes it really takes. I cannot exist forever in this state. How quickly I will be removed; how quickly I will be replaced.

Animal Rain

You are afraid this might mark the end of all the beauty in the world. Maybe you will be swept up in the rare, strange rains because anything can be unlikely until it happens to you. You are concerned the creatures will come down without guts or thoughts or heart and land with open, howling throats, that they will come for us agitated, ragged, dragging, their suddenly loosening skin suits mottled, rotting. Change has made them ugly in their own bodies. Ugly like me when they were beautiful like you. Next, it will get dark early. You want more from this. You want it to be a failure of imagination to not leave when you have the chance, to not be able to identify true trouble spots, to fall so far from home, and I do not know how to prepare for the coming endless restlessness of necessary questions, needed conversations, honest explanations. You don't know yet how to gather up storms, hold tight during updrafts, what can happen in intense low areas, but I do. You insist this phenomenon – all phenomena – only be about the wild discovery of natural beauty, but I know the cost of natural things, beautiful things: they become evidence; when you grow up, they haunt you.

The Endling

The death cabinet is under lock and key, so jimmy the thing open. Slide the card right in there and set free what is small and precious. Mother the last wonder of them all. Institutionalized, paralyzed, dizzy with sudden choices. It is singular. An ecosystem of one and one only singing for someone like itself – any single living being like itself – in the entire emptied world.

When the sun goes down, will it stay awake forever or get some sleep like the rest of us who are still reproducing, if only in fits and starts? Wake up cool to the possibility that it is the last of a kind: a mourning relict. It will make no more of it. It wants to be about bodies, but it is no longer about bodies.

Listen: it can see the future; there will be no genetic rescue. It calls out for itself – any living being like itself – howling through time, only steps from its last home.

Hummers

you know if you can hear it. a high hum is hum enough so you can catch
the edge of sound. it works at you; wears you down in all the delicate places.
anyone can catch a case of it, but most are immune somehow. a small percentage
of a lucky few of us can hear smell, too: a sniff of shorted out power; the slow burn
of soft brain; the kicky scent of electric death. can you hear what we hear? the nausea
of noise filtered through flattened foil caps or white fuzzy waves of radio or string
and plastic cup telephones broadcast in from the past before time or a world yet to come.

Catatonia

Lost inside: if you could, how you might, describe the insensibility underneath, but you are caught up in a miles-deep dream. Time curves around the wild truth of the nothing you are. I am here for the random chaos of a late stage miracle, the belief in a freak savior of your world. I sit frozen, alone, with your stare, the rigid tension of your bones, and wait.

Abulia

mush mind of nothing.
in this space, in the diminished outer limits,
there is no interior world, but
I am not dead: I can still taste the stars.

Part III:
Short History

Lesson

Tethered still by a necessary few grams to the Big Bang, that last switched-on moment buzzing with many particular futures, I use my cellular memory to ride the hot flow of matter, split the fitted curve, vibrate on various frequencies, travel on the muscular back of primal time in a looping line back to the long ago curly-haired girl licking soft cheese off a spoon in the harvest yellow kitchen the moment before it happens. Mid-loop, suspended in the same space, is the pot of hot water boiling on the stove.

She is an iota, a particle, an infinitesimal part of all this immensity, existing only in my near past, but, somehow, her two still full-skinned legs still kick under the old Formica table, feet rooting around trying to reach solid ground. I am myself space and time, but also solid in the physical world: I must move further, deeper, into the inevitable future. The violence of these passing through phases, the narrow margins, the places in between, this push to contain my chaos, cannot change what happens next.

Nothing to hear, just cosmic silence: skin burns quietly. Not much to see, just infinite starless darkness: skin burns quickly. Some of it sloughs off, and is, quite suddenly, strangely, cold to the touch. Events followed: ambulance called, blankets found, bandages procured. But there is no such thing as empty space: the first spike of pain opens me up. Fills each prehistoric cell. Bleeds into every fine granule in every single rough second. Peels back the dividing line and lays bare the unexamined, unimagined body without sheath, casing, skin. Riddled with paradoxes, with racked up violations, it will still not reveal the secrets it keeps.

Time has worked me hard. I cannot move ahead, go back; it loops just out of reach. Nothing left but the life-long thickened ribbing and mottled edges of a hairless hard leg-long scar. My organs might shift to accommodate how the heft of every grain of space in my organic bones forces radical change, but I am stuck with the same body I've always had, such a purgatory when there are so many others to inhabit: the dream of slipping into new skin dies here.

Pure O

I am made of meat, which the tongue monster loves because it is hungry. Inside me,
a grotesquerie of hormones, bluish fluids, virus, bacteria, congealed organic matter rough
to the touch and super-duper alive.
Thrill to the billions of biological mutations!
Here is one big nightmare tongue, that most moist and muscular of organs has turned
monster, slithering, searching for my brain. Licking, looking, for the secret
tunnels that crisscross my blood barrier and salty spinal fluid.

Study my smooth and scalloped gums for signs of rot. Examine
my extra-large tonsils for somewhere to swallow. Drag my jawbone
and break me open. I'll run away and join the legions of zig zag girls split
into ragged thirds. Insert me in the box for women sawed in half
for everyone's viewing pleasure.
The illusion rips me up; I try to hold myself together.

Who or what should I be?
Should I yell through the bullhorn: Behold a sideshow attraction body!
A carnival of feet jutting out of shoulders, hands dangling from knees. Untethered
shifty eyeballs. Dozens of dirty chins. A pre-rhinoplasty nose and
fifty pounds of tumor growing within.
Stick around for a bite to eat after the show. See if I taste when I lick my skin.
The tongue monster is here –
it will show itself in.

But sit tight because the motion of the circles will make you sick. It comes in
big looping loops like an O. Big, spacey holes,
especially the kind with a deep dark O like an O itself keep me cramping.
Deep Neanderthal squatting. Archaic human pain bearing down. Back to the days
when we were trembling. Back to the days when it was all dark
before the light. Back to the days before the burning. A hole of burning in the skin.
There it is! My original sin!
Never mind all that now.
The tongue monster is hungry –
it just wants in.

I gather myself up as I'm tripping down all around. Gather up
all my falling off parts, my jagged pointy parts, my pulling hair
and ripping lips parts, my big chunks of white and dark meat parts,
slippery yellow skin up on my bones.
Too many demands and the biological revulsion grows. The dissembling voices
making me beg for the cure! How do you learn to speak
when you have no words? They all fall out the bottom here. Can you feel
the tongue monster breathing heavy in your soft cartilage ears?

Strangertwin

My double walker walks the world looking for me. Her Pale of Settlement face
is, of course, mine, but my mild blindness keeps me guessing. On and on
she goes and goes. I see her face, but I don't. Her long ago hand like family
on the back of my neck. She is here for our moment. One cannot
stay alone on the planet for too long.
When my doppelgänger drops by for a midnight visit, I pay attention.

She smiles at me across the breadth of time, shifts into her organic state.
She is as lovely as I am just for me. I know her beginning, and also her end,
but I see only what she wants me to see. Not her rotten social six or
the ruined city of her body. Not surviving on little else but ersatz coffee
or last on the endless loop of a line for the gas.
She doesn't owe me anything, but she always finds me.

Our blood the only type on Earth; we are the same but different in and out
of her skin. Back in the Pale, we are lost and found. In the old country, I borrow
the muscle memory of her voice. I speak her loanword language, suddenly
fluent as the heavy jumble of words press my lips and tongue.
She lets me look around for comfort, others with our thoughts and faces,
but I forget what I cannot see.

In the morning, still sleepy with dreams of our demise, I realize
the length and depth of her journey. The back and forth of her bargaining.
The energy she spent for me. The pleas and prayers, the haggling up and down
for just a split second more, whatever needs to be done, however long it takes,
to keep it moving in the right direction to an accident of time and place
when another face will replace her.

The world moves on and on. No one knows how she goes. I've already had more
life than she's had, more than most, maybe more than I deserve.

Advanced Math

Who knew my added-up faults could summon the devil himself?! I had no idea that multiplication, division, the blame game of find the variable, the search for the perfect world of right answers previously denied to me, could lead to a direct line down to the underworld. Everyone knows I can't add or subtract, but I can still – do still – leap from place to place, cross dangerous thresholds, wary that stillness will be the beginning of my extinction story. Consider how my disastrous inability to put numbers together in any meaningful way has brought me here to this moment: Here I am! Also, how did I end up here?

Yes, math is unholy, but the doing of it, counting's active state, the manual labor of it, the busy-ness of it, the change in direction of it, is supposed to be an act of equilibrium –an expression, a proposition – but now all the devil has to do is collide probability with possibility – the probability of the possibility of no possibility at all! – because I am clearly in over my head. Uncertain if I sense his presence, I need to keep my half of my latest devil's bargain, but the whole idea of practice is absurd. How much good does practice do, how much good does counting do, when you are the invisible squared?

I move up to the front of the line because I am desperate for equanimity, but mostly I want permission to want, to have at it. Count me into existence! Count me in! Time minus time. Curve plus curve. Theorem begets theorem. The inflection point miles above my station, I am hard pressed to keep up more exhausting days of same. But I am way past the exit, the boundaries of proof; I no longer recognize truth. You either get it or you don't, so how do I get out?

This is where my curve changes, and I can't help but love the dirty world that raised me a little less. What it feels like for a body in trouble: a constant moving to the maximum. Get the devil down, get him down, get him back down! Find the way out, or risk never again feeling, knowing, the slippery smooth plane of peak undulation. Unable to find the rising point, there is little left but the falling, the inevitable descent down.

Open Poem to My Grifter

I owe you brain and breath, but I can't make good on it with so few years left. Caught up, as I am, in the strange tangle of your buying and selling world. Suddenly, in late life, I embraced the bracing shudder of sudden change and the clean break of stolen identity. Leave it to me to hold out for so long and still suffer an old-fashioned split, a breakdown, nervous or not, for such a simple scheme, such sly clever theft from such a confidence man. You have never been free, I have never been free, and now I know the life-changing pleasure of wanting, getting, what I can't afford, what doesn't belong to me.

I don't remember my past bodies, or how I was swindled into ending up in this one. How I owe you essential parts of this one; how I'll pay for this one. Perhaps all my previous forms were both rousing successes and abject failures, unperfect, too, and maybe I worked them past exhaustion, accepted every questionable invitation. It seems I freely joined your masquerade, even after my recent incarnation. So I go through the long process of being born and reborn in different forms. I grow and grow, become fully grown, in negative space, around and surrounding, defining, your negative space, where there was previously no space at all.

How you got me moving. How you got me on the make, thriving in the margins. How I made my way up the loyal ranks in your work the gap system. As if I didn't understand what you were into. As if I didn't understand all the expectations in your well-versed, expert seduction. I, fledgling, novice, stripped down to salt and meat, gristle in my teeth, expected to pay you back with interest. What I wanted was to be a thousand-year-old thing with muscular thigh-lines, everywhere feathers, giant mighty wings, but a true body is beyond reasonable reach from the other side: now there is no other way for you, for me, to stay alive.

Even with the debt I can't draw down. If you are hungry, I am hungry. An animal body is always hungry. It leaks, betrays, quietly celebrates the unquiet being somewhat more than halfway to the grave. This is where I'm going, too. So even now, you pull at me. Even now. I have learned nothing: I keep doing it.

Pact

Let's never speak of it again. Chalk it up to lesson learned: a universe all caught up in itself controls nothing. But every so often the blunt true force of *that thought* strikes and I am suddenly shook. What might have been, could have been, pulls me down, shakes me out. My oneling, in her solid singleton physical form, remains her maverick self, out wandering the world. *She is still here.*

There won't be a next time; I came home a humbled woman. You'll find me in the next phase of my surge, where errant electrical charges, and the metallic taste of potential tangible loss on my tongue, remind me I'm just energy. Made up of aching bits and pieces, twisted building blocks, alive and able elements. Baffled by the terrible, unknowable future. Ready to surrender to sacrifice, offer up sand and salt in massive hourglasses or what's in my own skull in my own smooth and empty head. Uneven bargains, whispered epiphanies, covenants sworn and kept. *I will live lightly after this.*

The animal within groans to life, searches far corners for the one who is of itself, who grew inside. No one else – *definitely not me* -- can be trusted. This is what is left: human-like middle space organs skirting past shady parts. It insists I consider the cost of my ongoing allegiance to multiple magical thoughts, the dissembling versions of why I appear and disappear, the way I was just humming along under clouds, under sky, under the deadly weight of the give and take of time, endlessly waiting for the inevitable fall and rise.

Everything comes back to that morning. You and I do not know what will happen, who goes next: the things we don't tell children. I went in wild, went in flailing, seizing on mixed signals. I came out questioning the world of my false face, my seemingly comfortable place nestled in the warm body of the mad universe, came out stripped, afflicted, stunned.

What have I done? What have I done?

Conundrum

Where is late last summer in time's new curve? All I want is to ebb and flow
with the violent bend of space and time back to the first warm days,
but the four laws won't let me.
We are all beholden to heat and temperature and energy and work. There was a before,
the past, but now we are in the present tense. What should I do
with all the hours left in all the days? Why is it today and not another day or the day before
that day or one of the last summer days in a summer past?
In the now, I am in this moment, but you are not here,
not there, not anywhere. Not anymore.
Not you. Not winner never wins: memorize this because it's true.
Now the curve and bend of time and the sun won't give you back to me.
Now can't be now, but the past was certainly then. Past tense and it will never
happen that way again.
The warm tomato and grass smell of late last summer and the soft city streetlights
and crossing the boulevard in the heat of the slow evening before it happened
--there is always a before-- and now and then it is the way it will never be again.

Polymath Girl Poem

Somebody get this girl a mother! She is gifted with thoughts, pushed up against madness. A half step from telepathy, not certain of her psychopathy, and somehow she feels she belongs to me but can't really belong to me. Like I'm her reincarnated mother come back to claim her. Like I've returned her mama conqueror. As if I have the power to name her.

She demands a different kind of honesty, but I'm so dry and thirsty and beaten and brought to both my knees. She knows what happened, what didn't happen, that day by the river. She's so polymathy in her my memories flicker.

What do you do with a girl like her? Send her to school? But she already knows! Tell her to learn? But she's already there! This gifted with clairvoyance girl somehow knows how I bowed down before that dirty river. She came looking for me, her mama savior, but I can no longer name her. This polymath girl is gifted with muscle memory, one of the never named she remains, yet she feels she belongs to me but can't really belong to me. Someone put her on the spectrum for me when she says she is the spitting image of me but how could she be? How could she belong to me?

But she does know me. She knows what happened, what didn't happen, that day by the river. Polymath girl, how you crave the river! The rhythmic pull of the river. The river will breathe for you, make your heart beat for you, think with your brain for you. The sad ringing song of the river will sing for you. All the clinking sea glass by the river shore will clink for you. The garbage river will exhale its filthy breath for you. You'll never be clean again, but how many times can I save you?

She demands a different kind of honesty, but I'm so tired and worn and dragged down to both my knees. I gift her a slow story, but she's so far ahead of me. Either I did or didn't have a daughter, but I can't be your mother because in the time it took you to find me someone else has already named me.

Flat Space

All my time jumping and electric wave surfing and space hitching got me to this long moment:
I find myself on this flat planet where you don't live.
Most humans can't exist here, so I don't blame your absence. Warm-blooded bodies
do not generally enjoy the crush from the third dimension into the exquisite second
where you are thin and flat and suddenly the other.
For me it is a relief.
The constant longing for a more elegant figure falls away. How else can I be at peace
with the pushing of flesh off my bones, which should hurt but doesn't. For a moment
I hum and quiver like a tuning fork, and it feels like love.

You are all the dark matter no one else can see, but you can't be home and here:
that is both hidden and simple. Your desire for structure, to be corporeal – you don't care much
for the shimmer or the shape shift – is as intense as my need to shed thousand-year-old skin.
What good is all the chaos if I collapse into myself. If I burn out star-like. But from friction
comes heat, and there are dimensions, other dimensions, too straight, too square, too absurd
for even me to see.

Now and then I'll visit you back in round world. You know the way I mimic
the give and take of conversation. I can curve and bend and undulate with the best
of them. Understand that I will always fool them all. Look for me in little bits of uninhabited
space. I'll spy and learn and listen in with the flies on the walls.

Crazy For Two

What kind of gaze you give under brightest middle of the night diner lights
in the smallest moments. Start talking, and I'll gift you the truth of me
showing you mine. We are already drunk, but definitely order more
purple teeth wine. Also, turkey clubs on toast and a long bottle of still water.
How we drink and feed ourselves so we are full.

What's going on here is we don't say it and don't say it because synchronicity
is that we both see the searing fresh trouble it will bring. The singleness of this one
night out of zillions, twelve hours shoved into one shift, which does nothing
but curve the world away from us. The bells chime, swinging crazily back and forth,
all the alarms go off, but what is set in motion is already in motion.

You dare me down; I'm known to take all bets and entertain all comers. Still,
I get up off the killing floor and mad dash to the exit while you sharpen
your slicing knives. The inevitable slaughter is more than I bargained for,
but I stop dead at the door. I am also unhinged; we are a pair of terminal cases.
Take a damp napkin and wipe the dark blood off my dirty face.

Our meal is here. There are no other choices, so pour the wine. Just this one night
in this booth under these lights so there will never be another. Drink the dry mouth
wine and ubiquitous diner water. Toast the two of us who sit here in this moment
eating sandwiches constructed layer by layer by layer. Then there will be a bill to pay
and other nights to live through.

Start talking; tell me everything. We'll go crazy on each other:
I am here for it, as they say. Stab my surface layer with the sharp gaze
of deep-set eyes on your fingertips, and then a little deeper.

Origin Story

I was young, not yet named, and super cool, you know, so I went where you'd go down to the party part of the old-world City. The City liked me dirty, expected my confession, demanded my redemption. Motherless, unmoored, wild to the trained eye, restless in my bones, easily flattered, taken in by the promise of magic. Mouth dry and powdery, feeling so loose I might've spun off into space, but I stood there with my violence and my sword for cutting and my nameless face. Unnamed, I named myself.

I was hunting, and every day was Feast Day. It was the end of the last summer before the first fall. All the men and more men and more with their deviled egg faces and boiled sausage fingers, all drunk with house red dirty mouths and bewildered John the Baptist faces. Entertainment in those days were beheadings in the evenings: sword, of course, not guillotine. Some people get to do whatever they choose, but I was raised to be the dancing daughter. Barefoot, braceleted, draped in silver and smooth precious stones. Only a matter of time until all I wanted was to draw blood, break bones. This dance, this ceremony, how I was in the world: on my hands like a gypsy, on my feet but quivering, on my stomach and unveiled.

I descended down to the City under the stairs, way, way down to a sliver of a silent space in a vast warren of a place. Tunnels twisting this way and that. Pipes of cool soil coiled around and around and around. Thirsty in the back of the throat. Hair knotted thick to the scalp. Red dirt under square filed nails. A young man offered me a joint of nerve gas sweet smoke spiked with white dust: did I want to party or what? Somehow he knew what I craved. The ugly aching beauty of a severed head, surprised eyes, an astonished face on the wall for all to see, another notch on my head-belt, and a trophy for me. I thought nobody was a murderer like me. Got muscular like me. Found breathless grunting strength like me. Who needs whose permission to leave? He held the door open for me.

How do you know who is the devil and who is the savior? You don't. The greatest riddle ever told: did I choose him, or did he choose me? Still, wrap up his perishable head and keep his cold lips fresh for me. Just a young woman and a man's head on a plate: nothing else here to see. He was the epitome of eyes everywhere, both the light and the darkness. He didn't look the way you think he might: such unvarnished beauty. His face chiseled marble; a church worship statue face. A bright morning star. Pupiled eyes, wavy hair, a stone magnificent body. His wrinkled and unfurled robes folded in all the right places. A museum piece, once quite alive, but no longer, and not for a long, long time.

I didn't know what was ahead of it, the future of it. I couldn't recognize a world disappearing; I've never understood confession. When I heard whispering in my ear, I freely entered the conversation: there is no other explanation. Things get lost. People, too. The world was waiting, and it has little patience for poor mortals, peasant girls, smoking something with a stranger under the stairs of the City.

The texture of his mind in mine was new, but I did understand the cost of his bargain. The smell of smoke, sweet cancerous air, exhaled by one who is a watcher, who has been cast out, who has, quite clearly, fallen. I inhaled, and realized, was suddenly aware of, the truth of the next moment even before it happened, even before the flipped feel of losing grip on time itself: I will fall, too. Where once my two feet were solid on the ground, the horizon line, my eye-level, turned around, upside down. The sky meets the sea meets the soft soil. Into the abyss, like others newly named, destined to wake up alone. He knows me, either I chose him, or he chose me, but this was an imprint of my existence in the universe. I got out. When I lost the world, hit the floor, I knew I wouldn't forget and wouldn't forget that I will outlive them all.

I woke up alone. Alone like a sudden exodus, a calamity, catastrophe, a complete extinguishing of all except one. Not a single other person in the breathing City, but then the walls exhaled; the release such a spectacular sound. Some blood on my face. Lips: split, sore. Nose: soft but solid. Body: slightly tender, bruised. Spoons, shots, spilled bottles, rolled bills all proof that he is still here somewhere. Time moved forward, but I lost my violence, my sword. The weight of what was coming: significant rupture, howling loss, the bad nights were still far into the future; in that moment, I could leave, and I was all the lightness in the world.

The City and I were so young. Even then I knew there was no real way up, or back. These days, I dream of time in irregular lines, angles measured, marked off: the jagged edges at the end of existence. Once I was born, but after the first conversion, remained unnamed. I started living, have been alive all this time. Alive without redemption, like the City, but he cuts through the noise of the world with my grand bargain, my dirty exchange. The devil is in the details, so when I slip back through the door, I can see my beginning, also my end, and I know the way I knew it once and never will again.

For Zoë: You are my little love and my heart. You are singular, and you are everything. I love the way you embrace your sense of humor and your wild imagination. I love your stories. I love telling you stories. I love the way we teach each other about important things. I love spending time with you. "I love you more than the world."

For Joel: You & I have always been committed to offering each other unconditional encouragement and support in all our creative work. It is an inextricable part of the way we love each other. You never give up on me, and you don't let me give up on myself. I treasure our relationship. You are magnificent, and I love you very much.

For my parents: Thank you for giving me the space to discover my own interests, for not micro-managing my reading choices, and for encouraging my relationship with stories, with history, with theater. What wonderful gifts! It has all mattered more than you know. I love you both. Thank you for how you care about me. Thank you for your love.

For Carol and Dick: Thank you for showing me how to be a writer and a teacher. Thank you for the many opportunities and advice you have shared with me over the years. Thank you for your endless love and support.

For Susan, Dan, & Luca & Marco: Your friendship, your guidance, and your love means everything to me. We are more than just family. Our vacations and visits have always been the best of times, especially the ones with the kids. I cannot thank you enough for all the long conversations, your advice, and your support.

Thank you to my life-long friends from SUNY Plattsburgh, AMDA, and Brooklyn College. I adore you all, and I am so happy we have been able to stay in touch! Yay for social media! Being able to share my poems/stories with all of you has been a significant part of the joy of publishing my work. Also, thank you to all my friends who read my work and say nice things. Thank you so much for your love and support! I appreciate it more than I can really explain.

For Morgan M. X. Tayu-Schulz: These poems, and most of the creative work I have finished in the last 20+ years, would not exist without you. This is the truth. You are a generous reader, an amazing writer, and a great friend.

Thank you to the editors of these wonderful journals where these poems first appeared:

Anti-Heroin Chic: "Origin Story"

Coffin Bell Journal: "Sex Fat", "Gone Toxo", "Wild Evolution", "Creation Play", "Pure O"

Exquisite Pandemic: "The Kissing Disease", "In Native State", "Advanced Math", "In the Evening, During Quarantine"

Hamilton Stone Review: "Strangertwin", "Virus Poem", "Crazy for Two", "Half-Life"

Hole in the Head Review: "Physical System"

Little Somethings Press: "The Endling"

Newtown Literary: "Vestalia", "Conundrum"

On the Seawall: "Virus Child", "Open Poem to My Grifter"

Otis Nebula: "Microchimera", "Flat Space"

Planisphere Quarterly: "Lesson", "Unscientific Study", "Animal Rain"

Rogue Agent Journal: "The Call of the Void"

St. Katherine Review: "Quotidian Fever"

The Avenue Journal: "Late Hour"

Wild Roof Journal: "Pact"

Naomi Bess Leimsider has published poems, flash fiction, and short stories in The Avenue Journal, Booth, Anti-Heroin Chic, Wild Roof Journal, Planisphere Quarterly, Little Somethings Press, Syncopation Literary Journal, On the Seawall, St. Katherine Review, Exquisite Pandemic, Orca, Hamilton Stone Review, Rogue Agent Journal, Coffin Bell Journal, Hole in the Head Review, Newtown Literary, Otis Nebula, Quarterly West, The Adirondack Review, Summerset Review, Blood Lotus Journal, Pindeldyboz, 13 Warriors, Slow Trains, Zone 3, Drunkenboat, and The Brooklyn Review.

She has been a finalist for the Acacia Fiction Prize, the Saguaro Poetry Prize, and the Tiny Fork Chapbook Contest. In addition, she received a Pushcart Prize nomination in 2022.

She teaches creative and expository writing at Hunter College/CUNY

Also Available from Cathexis Northwest Press:

Something To Cry About
by Robert Krantz

Suburban Hermeneutics
by Ian Cappelli

God's Love Is Very Busy
by David Seung

that one time we were almost people
by Christian Czaniecki

Fever Dream/Take Heart
by Valyntina Grenier

The Book of Night & Waking
by Clif Mason

Dead Birds of New Zealand
by Christian Czaniecki

The Weathering of Igneous Rockforms in High-Altitude Riparian Environments
by John Belk

If A Fish
by George Burns

How to Draw a Blank
by Collin Van Son

En Route
by Jesse Wolfe

sky bright psalms
by Temple Cone

Moonbird
by Henry G. Stanton

southern athiest. oh, honey
by d. e. fulford

Bruises, Birthmarks & Other Calamities
by Nadine Klassen

Wanted: Comedy, Addicts
by AR Dugan

They Curve Like Snakes
by David Alexander McFarland

the catalog of daily fears
by Beth Dufford

Shops Close Too Early
by Josh Feit

Vanity Unfair and Other Poems
by Robert Eugene Rubino

Destructive Heresies
by Milo E. Gorgevska

Bodies of Separation
by Chim Sher Ting

The Night with James Dean and Other Prose Poems
by Allison A. deFreese

About Time
by Julie Benesh

Suspended
by Ellen White Rook

The Unempty Spaces Between
by Louis Efron

Quomodo probatur in conflatorio
by Nick Roberts

Call Me Not Ishmael but the Sea
by J. Martin Daughtry

Coming To Terms
by Peter Sagnella

Acta
by Patrick Wilcox

Cathexis Northwest Press

www.ingramcontent.com/pod-product-compliance
Lightning Source LLC
Chambersburg PA
CBHW050333120526
44592CB00014B/2168